Patterns for Patchwork
Quilts and Cushions

Patterns for Patchwork Quilts and Cushions

Suzy Ives

B T Batsford Ltd London

For May Hawksley with love

© Suzy Ives 1977
First published 1977
ISBN 0 7134 0095 1

Printed in Great Britain by
Butler and Tanner Limited, Frome and London
for the publishers
B T Batsford Ltd
4 Fitzhardinge Street
London W1H OAH

Contents

Acknowledgment

I would like to thank Charlotte Gerlings for her constant help with the design and ideas for this book, and Thelma M Nye, my editor, without whom none of it would have made sense. Also a great Thank You to Suzan Farmer for her patience in checking my designs.

Suzy Ives
Willesden 1977

Introduction

This is a book of patterns for patchwork quilts and cushions. The measurements are of necessity approximate and are given in both metric and imperial. Because of the difficulty in expressing exact metric equivalents for imperial measures, if a pattern is to be measured in millimetres, use only the metric instructions: if in feet and inches, use only the imperial instructions.
Always check the size given for the finished quilt against the bed for which it is to be made. Some of the quilts have an overhang and others do not. In some patterns the number of patches needed look daunting, but remember, a large quilt will become a family heirloom and will take a very long time to make. You do not have to prepare all the patches at once, but do make sure that you will have enough fabric to complete the quilt.
For beginners to the craft of patchwork it is advisable to start with the simpler cushion patterns and then move on to the quilts.

Tools

Scissors and cutting tools
A pair of very sharp scissors for cutting fabric
An equally sharp pair for cutting paper only
Pinking shears for cutting fabrics that tend to fray badly
A small pointed pair of scissors for cutting loose ends of cotton and unpicking short seams
A scalpel or craft knife for cutting templates
A seam ripper for undoing long seams.

Needles
Straw needles for tacking cotton patches to the papers
Sharps 8, 9 and 10 for sewing the patches together and for quilting (the finer the fabric, the finer the needle)
Glover's needles for sewing leather and suede
(Some people prefer 'Betweens' for sewing the patches together.)

Pins
Glass headed pins, for pinning the papers to the patches and for
pinning any interlining layers to the finished patchwork. Pins
with a glass head tend to be sharper and more slender than
dressmakers pins. They are also very easy to use and less likely to
get lost in the work.
Silk pins, for use with silk patchwork and very fine fabrics.

Templates
These can be bought in many shapes and sizes, made from either plastic or
metal. It is often, however, necessary to make your own templates, and this
is most easily done with stiff card or perspex. The shape of the template
must be cut out with a scalpel and it is essential that the template is absolutely
accurate. Even the slightest inaccuracy will cause the finished patchwork to
be puckered or rumpled.
Papers are cut from the template. Window templates are pairs of templates.
The larger one is used for cutting the fabric (with accurate turnings) and the
smaller used for cutting the papers. Window templates are useful if the
fabric used for the patch has a motif or pattern that needs centring.

Sewing threads
Mercerised cotton in 40, 50 or 60 thickness (match the thickness of the
thread to the thickness of the patch fabric).
Pure silk thread for sewing silk patchwork.
Tacking cotton.

Graph papers
These are very useful when planning patchwork.
Squared paper is used for triangular, square, rectangular and random
patchwork and isometric paper for hexagonal, diamond shaped, lozenge
shaped, 'coffin shaped' and long hexagon patchwork.
Although it is expensive to use the graph paper for the actual papers of the
patches, it is often a way of making absolutely accurate papers.

Pressing
A steam iron and a pressing cloth.

Suitable fabrics

Almost all fabrics can be used for patchwork, provided that all the patches in a piece of work are of approximately the same weight. If it is necessary to include a lightweight patch in a heavy piece of work, for reasons of colour or texture, then the lighter patch can be lined with *Vilene*, calico or cotton, to bring it up to the required weight. This interlining is cut to the same size and shape as the fabric for the patch and the two layers of fabric are then treated as one.

A large ragbag of scraps is easily collected, and it is helpful if they are stored in batches of colours and weights.

The following fabrics are all suitable for patchwork:

cotton, linen, lawn, cotton lawn, terylene lawn, silks (of all weights), velvets (cotton and silk velvet is more easily handled for patchwork than synthetic velvet), corduroy, felt, wool, suede, satin, brocade, PVC, and calico (eminently suitable).

Knitted or stretch fabrics, or fabrics that fray badly are unsuitable.

If any of the fabrics chosen are not pre-shrunk they should be washed and ironed dry before use.

Try not to mix washable fabrics with fabrics that must be dry cleaned or fast-dyes with dyes that might run.

Press all fabrics before using them.

Making templates

Materials
Firm card (thickness of 3 postcards)
A ruler and metal straight edge
A pair of compasses and protractor
A very sharp pencil
Scalpel or craft knife.

Work on a firm, even surface. As far as possible, look directly down onto the ruler and protractor when measuring. Keep the pencil sharp and check all measurements twice.

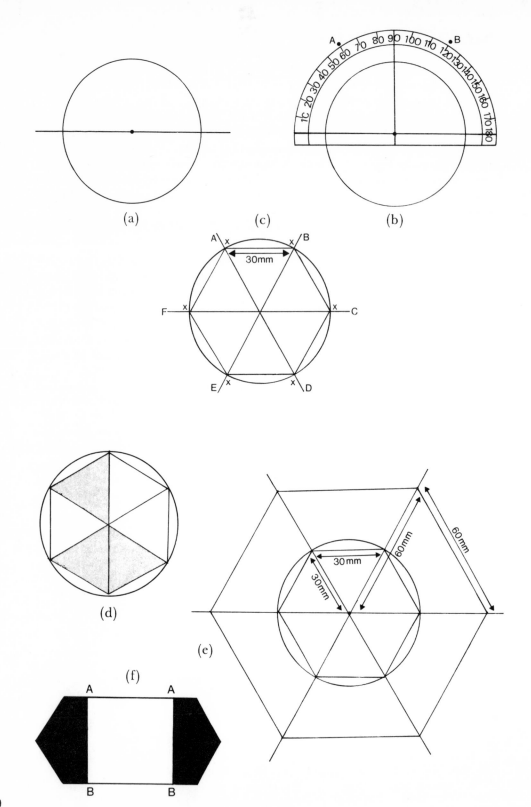

(a)

(c)

(b)

(d)

(e)

(f)

Hexagon

Draw a circle with 30 mm (1 in.) radius on the card. Then, using the ruler, draw a straight line through the centre of the circle, extending it each side, figure (a) below.

Place the protractor with the centre of the base line and the centre of the circle matching, figure (b) below.

Mark off 60 degrees and 120 degrees above the base line (points A and B); turn the protractor round and do the same below the base line (points D and E). The centre line is F–C, figure (c) below.

Join points A, B, D and E to the centre, F and C are already joined, see also figure (c).

Mark the points where the lines cross the circle with an x. Using the ruler, join up all the points x to form a hexagon with 30 mm (1 in.) sides, again see figure (c)

Check all the sides are equal and cut the hexagon from the card with a craft knife.

Hexagons with sides of any length can be drawn using this method. If the basic circle has a radius of 60 mm (2 in.), the points will be marked on the edge of the circle and the sides of the hexagon will be 60 mm (2 in.), figure (d) opposite. Diamond-shaped and triangular templates can also be cut from the basic hexagon, figure (e) opposite.

Long hexagons

Draw a hexagon with sides of the required length. Cut the hexagon in half from straight side to straight side (between points A and B, see shaded portions on figure (f)). Draw a square with sides equal to AB. Stick the two halves of the hexagon to opposite sides of the square and redraw the new shape from the altered templates, figure (f) above.

Making papers

Materials
Template
Sharp pencil
Sharp scissors (for paper)
Sharp scissors (for fabric if the papers are to be made from *Vilene* or *Pellon*)
Magazine covers or stiff notepaper.

Place the template onto the paper and draw round it with a sharp pencil. Take care to keep the pencil at a right angle to the paper. This ensures that the pencil point is as close to the edge of the template as possible. Cut out the paper along the pencil outline. After cutting several papers, test their accuracy by matching up their sides. Discard any papers that are not completely accurate.

Papers that will be left in the finished work
These are made from iron-on *Vilene* or interlining. They are made in exactly the same way as ordinary papers.

Preparing the patches

Materials
Fabric, well pressed
Papers
Sharp scissors for cutting fabric only
Glass headed pins
Tacking cotton.

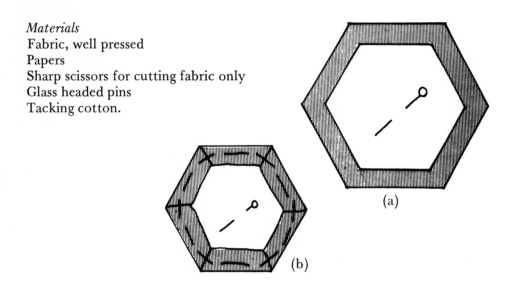

(a)

(b)

Pin the papers to the wrong side of the fabric with at least 30 mm (1 in.) clearance all round each paper.
Cut out the fabric to the same shape as the patch but allow 15 mm (½ in) turning allowance all round the patch, figure (a).
Fold the turning allowance over the edges of the patch and tack it down, figure (b). Do not use a knot in the cotton, because when the papers are removed the tacking cotton will pull out more easily.
Prepare all the patches necessary for the work before joining is begun.

Joining the patches

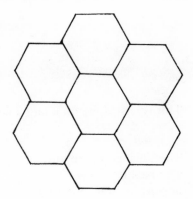

Materials
Prepared patches
Needle (sharps 8 to 10)
Sewing cotton
Small sharp scissors.

Take two patches and place them right sides facing.
Fill the needle with no more than 380 mm (15 in.) of sewing cotton and insert
the needle through both patches close to the edge of the seam.
Taking tiny oversewing stitches, sew along the edge of the patch. Take care that
the stitches are tiny and not too far apart. Always pass the needle through the
fabrics at right angles to the edge and do not pull the thread up too tightly. If
you pull too hard this will cause the join to pucker and the finished patchwork
will not lie flat. At the end of the first edge, leave the thread whole and place
another patch, right sides facing, along the next side. Continue sewing as shown
in the figures below.
When enough patches have been joined, fasten the final thread off very securely,
by stitching back for a few stitches. Press the patchwork on the wrong side. Pull
out the tacking threads that hold in the papers.
Remove the papers carefully, for these can be used again.
Press the patchwork again and re-tack round the folded turnings at the edge of
the patchwork.

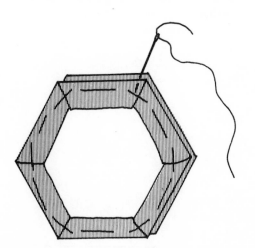
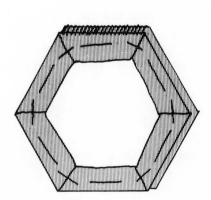

Mounting finished patchwork

This is best done on a large, clean, flat surface.

Materials
The finished patchwork
The backing fabric
Sewing cotton to match the main colours in the patchwork
Needle (9 sharps)
Fine steel or glass headed pins
Iron and ironing board
Pressing cloth.

Press the finished patchwork and the backing fabric carefully.
Place the patchwork, right side up, onto the backing fabric and smooth it out from the centre so that both fabrics are lying absolutely flat.
Pin the centre patch to the backing fabric.
Working outwards, pin all the patches down in turn, making sure that the patchwork lies absolutely flat and that there are no wrinkles in it or the backing fabric. Do not stretch either the patchwork or the backing fabric.
When the pinning is completed, fill the needle with the same colour thread as the patchwork and begin to 'tie' down the patchwork.

Tying
Pass the needle from behind the backing fabric, through both the backing fabric and the patchwork and out. (Leave 102 mm (4 in.) of thread behind the backing fabric.) The needle should come out on the patchwork side at the corner of the patch to be tied, at the point where the tiny oversewing stitches join it to the next patch.
Return the needle through the patch, only a tiny distance from the first needle hole. Tie the two loose ends of the thread that are under the backing fabric, in a reef knot (left thread over right, right thread over left).
Tie down the patches at regular intervals.
Tack round the edges of the patchwork and remove all the pins.
Press the 'tied' patchwork carefully, using a dry pressing cloth.
Hem down the edges of the patchwork.
Remove all the tacking and press again.

Quilts

Quilts are generally made in blocks or sections, which are then joined up to complete the quilt. When the patchwork is finished and joined, it is pressed, the tacking and papers are removed and the quilt is lined and interlined if necessary.

The backing of the quilt should be of a non-slip fabric, such as calico or cotton sheeting. Even an old blanket will do.

The interlining, which is added for warmth, is usually made of *Domette* (a fluffy fabric) or terylene wadding, but again, worn blankets are equally suitable.

If an interlinging is used, the three layers of the quilt (patchwork, interlining and backing) are quilted. This is done by hand with running stitch or back-stitch, or a fairly long straight stitch on the machine. If the quilt is more for decoration than warmth, there is no need for the interlining, and the quilt may be simply 'tied' to the backing fabric.

Backing the quilt

Place the finished patchwork face down onto the backing fabric and join the quilt to the backing fabric at the edges. This can be done along the fold that marks the outer turnings of the patchwork.

Leave a gap in the stitching on one edge of the quilt that will be large enough to turn the quilt through right side out.

The patchwork is tied to the backing as described in the section on mounting (page 14).

Interlining

The interlining is cut to the same size as the quilt and placed between the backing and the patchwork. The edges of the quilt can be bound with straight tape or simply joined as before.

Quilting

This is commenced at the centre of the patchwork and worked outwards towards the edges, taking care to keep the layers of fabric unwrinkled. The edges of the patchwork and backing are joined *after* quilting to prevent them from puckering. The joining is done by turning the edges of the backing fabric under and hemming them to the folded edges of the outer patches.

While making the quilt, it is easier if the papers from the centre of each block are removed as each block is completed. These papers can be used for the other blocks if they are not too worn.

Colour planning

Much of the charm of patchwork lies in the way the colours of the patches are arranged. Early patchwork was often a method for making use of scraps of fabric from old clothes or furnishings and therefore colour was used in a fairly random way. This can be effective, giving a somewhat kaleidoscopic feeling to the work but it can also seem muddled and confusing. Colour used in an ordered, though not rigid way gives the finished work a sense of balance and design which when combined with beautiful stitching makes patchwork an interesting and exciting form of fine needlework.

One colour work
Here the colour is limited to one colour only but interest is created by the use of varying shades of that colour, either from pale to dark or by using all the possible tones: for example, red can be graded from palest pink to darkest maroon, or the complete range of reds can be used, from palest pink again, through the orange reds and brown reds, to maroon and the purple red range.
The fact that all the shades used are directly related to each other gives the work a common factor and the work will appear co-ordinated.

Two colour work
Here the colour is limited to two colours and any shades produced by mixing the two. For example, yellow and blue as basic colours with green as the mixture.

Complementary colours
Here the two colours are complementary to each other and so each throws the other into prominence. For example, blue and brown, orange and pink, pink and green, yellow and purple. Here, each colour is equally dominant and the shift of interest from one to the other gives an almost sparkling effect.

Random colour
The use of a wide and varied range of colours can be balanced by taking the background colour as a unifying base. For this reason, the background should be of a fairly neutral shade, although some quite startling effects can be created by using one of the dominant colours in the patchwork. Patterned backgrounds can appear confusing with random colour work and so perhaps should be avoided in very colourful schemes.

Texture

The use of highly-textured fabrics with smooth or soft fabrics as a foil can be very effective indeed. Corduroy, wool, velvet, satin, silk, lace, suede, lawn, cotton and embossed fabrics can be mixed to give exciting results. The lighter weight fabrics can be lined to bring them up to the weight of the heavier fabrics.

Rose point patchwork
sometimes called Orange Peel patchwork

I have included this method of patchwork which, although it appears intricate and difficult, is in fact one of the easiest and most effective techniques. The joy of it is that no templates are required, nor tacking and the fabric for the pieces is simply torn to size. The best way of using it is for quilts and cushion covers since the finished fabric needs no lining or inter-lining, and is sturdy and serviceable while looking charmingly dainty. Choose fabrics that tear easily along the grain (both weft and warp); for example; calico, cotton, lawn, silk, linen.

A   B

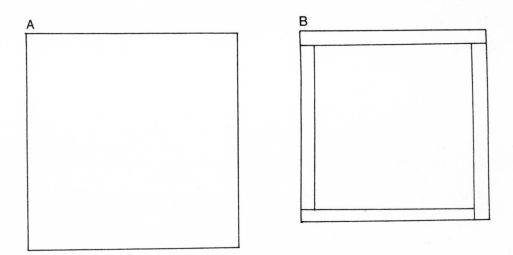

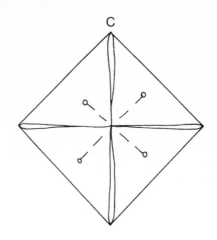

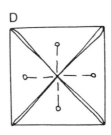

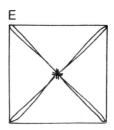

Method
Tear the basic fabric into 229 mm (9 in.) squares (A), measure these
carefully. The basic fabric is usually plain, but there is no reason why
patterns should not be used.

Press the squares carefully and with the iron make 6 mm (¼ in.) turnings on
all sides (B).

Fold the corners of the square to the centre, pin them into place (C).

Fold the corners of the new square into the centre, remove the pins and use
them to join the new corners (D).

Join the centre points of the squares with tiny stitches (E).

Make up at least four of these folded squares at a time.

Join the squares to one another as in ordinary patchwork in multiples of
four.

18

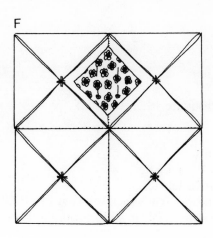

F

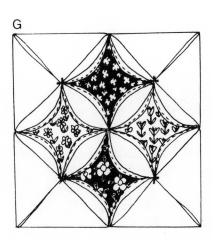

G

Tear the inlay fabric into 72 mm (2½ in.) squares and pin them to the basic fabric patches (F).

Fold the edges of the basic square (those showing around the edges of the inlay fabric) back over the inlay square. Hold them down with your thumb, you will see that these form a natural curve.

Sew these edges down with tiny running stitches. Sew through all the layers. Remove the pins from the inlay square.

19

Cushion A

Size: 500 mm (18 in.) square when finished.

Materials
¼ m (¼ yd) black fabric
⅕ m (⅕ yd) fine patterned fabric
Scraps of other patterned fabrics
⅝ m (⅝ yd) backing fabric. It is suggested that black fabric should be used in which case this amount of fabric will be enough for both the patches and the backing.

Patches   See key
All patches are 60 mm (2 in.) square.
Prepare 81 papers

Making up
Join the patches as shown. Make up the cushion cover.

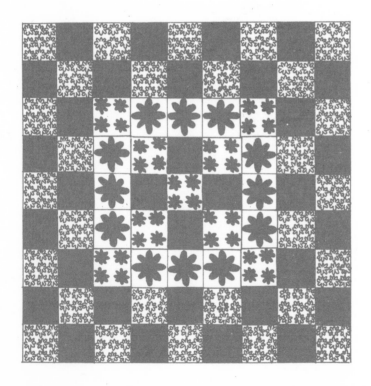

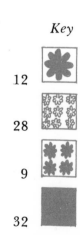

Key

12

28

9

32

Cushion B

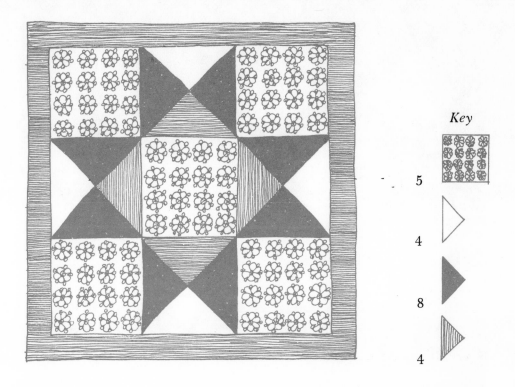

Key

5

4

8

4

Size: The patchwork is applied to a made up cover 400 mm (16 in.) square.

Materials
¼ m (¼ yd) patterned fabric
Scraps of other fabrics patterned and/or plain.

Patches   See key
Prepare 9 papers each 127 mm (5 in.) square.
Divide 4 of the papers diagonally into quarters.

Making up
Join the patches as shown. Mount onto the cushion cover.

Cushion C

16

4

32

16

16

Size: 500 mm (18 in.) square when finished

Materials
¼ m (¼ yd) large pattern fabric
Scraps of other fabrics patterned and/or plain
⅝ m (⅝ yd) backing fabric. It is suggested that the large patterned fabric should be used.

Patches
Prepare 36 papers each 76 mm (3 in.) square. Divide 16 papers diagonally into quarters (84 papers altogether).
See key

Making up
Join patches as shown. Make up the cushion.

Cushion D

Size: Make cushion cover 364 mm (14 in.) square.

Materials
¼ m (¼ yd) dark fabric
Scraps of other patterns.

Patches   See key
Prepare 13 papers each 60 mm (2 in.) square. Divide 2 diagonally in half and 10 diagonally into quarters.
Prepare 16 papers each 30 mm (1 in.) square
Prepare 4 42 mm (1⅝ in.) squares
Prepare 16 oblong papers each 30 mm x 60 mm (1 in. x 2 in.) and fold one corner of each as shown in figure (a) below.
Prepare the patches as shown in the key.

Making up
Join patches as shown. Mount onto the cushion cover.

Key

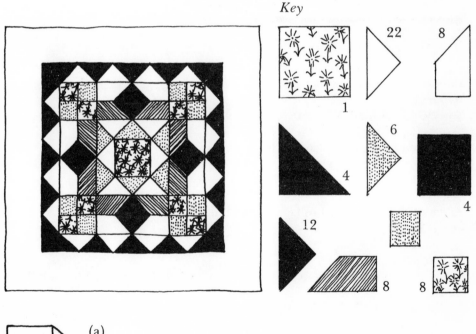

(a)

Cushion E

Size: 400 mm (16 in.) square when finished.

Materials
¼ m (¼ yd) plain fabric
Large scraps of other patterned fabrics
¼ m (½ yd) dark heavy cotton for backing fabric
Border made from 2 m (66 in.) of 60 mm (2 in.) wide ribbon.

Patches
20 papers 50 mm (2 in.) square, divided diagonally to give 80
triangular papers.

Making up
Cut a 125 mm (5 in.) square of patterned fabric, turn the edges in 12 mm
(½ in.).
Do the same to a 175 (7 in.) square of large patterned fabric and to a
225 mm (9 in.) square of plain fabric.
Lay the small square diamond-wise on the middle-size square then tack and
machine stitch into place.
Centre the middle-size square onto the largest square, tack and machine
stitch into place.

Make up the triangular patches in pairs using scrap fabrics. Join them in opposing pairs to make 20 squares.

Sew the squares together into 2 strips of 6 squares and a further 2 strips of 4 squares.

Sew these strips round the central square.

Attach the border ribbon. Mitre the corners.

Cushion F

Size: 400 mm (16 in.) square when finished.

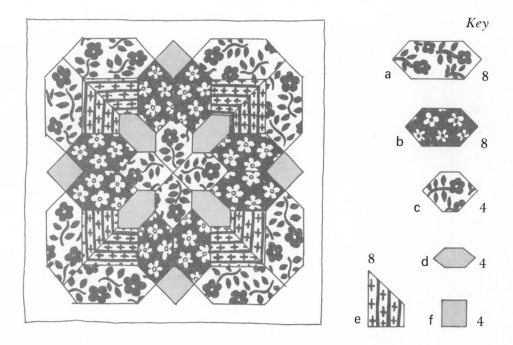

Materials

Large scraps of patterned fabrics

½ mm (½ yd) backing fabric — make into a 400 mm (16 in.) square cushion cover.

Making up
Join the patches as shown. Mount onto the made cushion cover.

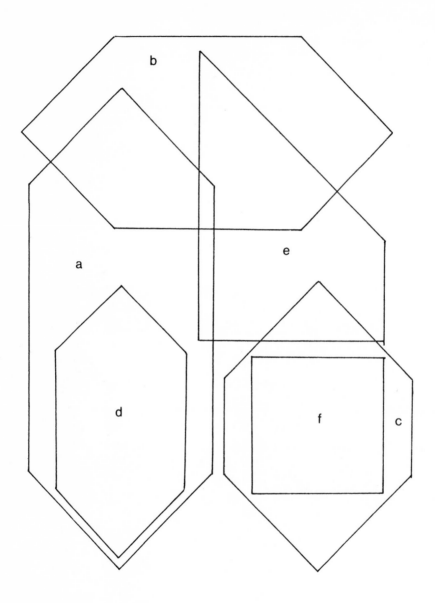

Cushion G

Size: 700 mm (24 in) square when finished.

Materials
¼ m (¼ yd) pale fabric }
⅛ m (⅛ yd) dark fabric } these are for the decorated strips.
Scraps of other patterned fabrics
5½ m (6 yd) of straight tape for the decoration and the piping
¾ m (¾ yd) backing fabric.

Patches
Prepare these papers
32 squares with 75 mm (3 in.) sides
4 strips each 75 mm x 300 mm (3 in. x 12 in.)
4 strips each 225 mm x 37 mm (9 in. x 1½ in.)
24 squares with 37 mm (1½ in.) sides
9 squares with 50 mm (2 in.) sides
16 squares with 52 mm (2 in.) sides, divide 8 of these into quarters.

There is no pattern key for this cushion as it uses up scraps of fabrics. The exploded diagram shows how it is assembled.

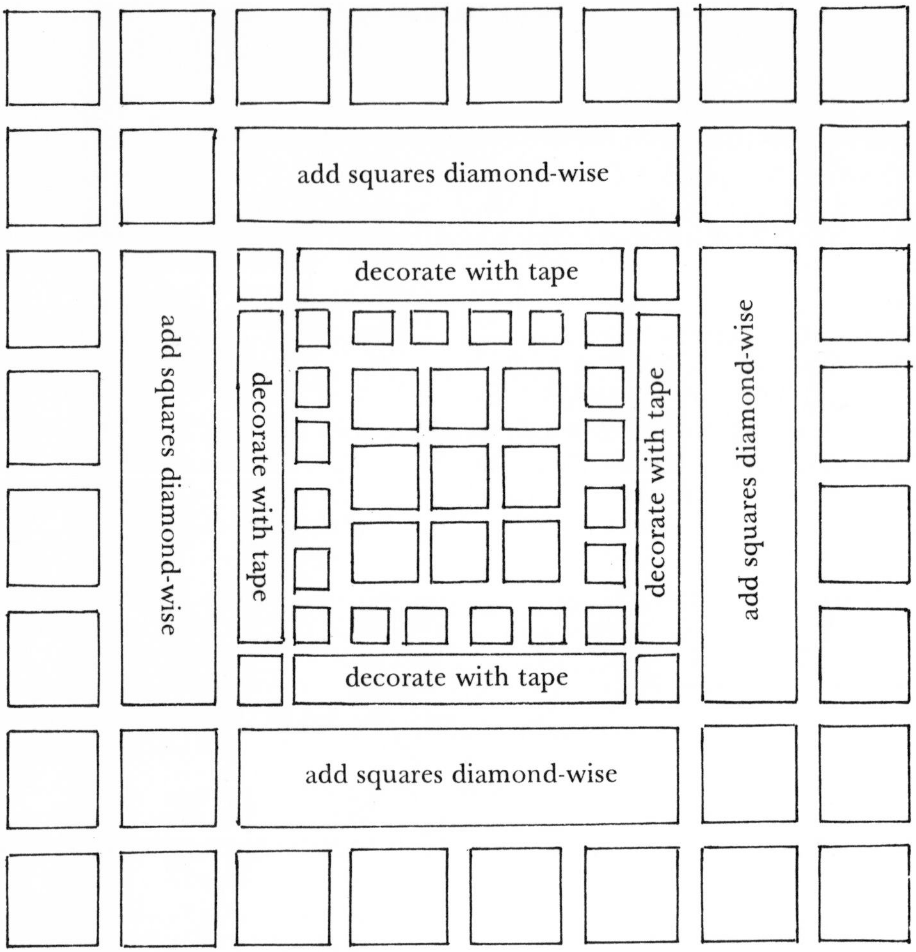

Making up
Join the patches as shown. Trim the narrowest strip with the tape as shown. Make up the cushion.

Cushion H

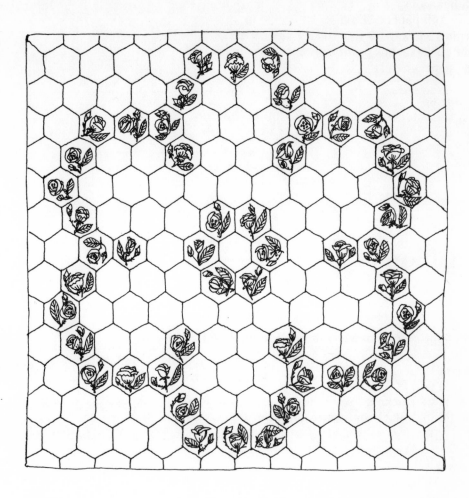

Key

  101 24 14

Size: 500 mm (18 in.) square when finished.

Materials
¾ m (¾ yd) plain fabric
⅜ m (⅜ yd) patterned fabric
⅝ m (⅝ yd) backing fabric.

Patches   See key
Using a hexigon made from a circle, radius 28 mm (⅞ in.)
Prepare
168 hexagons
Leave 149 papers whole
Divide 12 hexagons side to side (24 papers)
Divide 7 hexagons point to point (14 papers)
(187 papers in all)

Making up
Join the patches as shown. Make up the cushion.

Cushion I

Size: approx. 500 mm x 550 mm (18 in. x 20 in.)

Materials
½ m (½ yd) black fabric
¼ m (¼ yd) ticking
¼ m (¼ yd) black and white gingham.

Patches   See key
Prepare
55 small hexagons made from a circle, radius 28 mm (⅞ in.)
7 hexagons made from a circle, radius 88 mm (3½ in.)
6 diamonds made from a circle, radius 88 mm (3½ in.) as shown on page 11
1 large hexagon (for the backing) made from a 266 mm (10½ in.) circle (cut
the fabric for this 12 mm (½ in.) larger than the paper to allow for seams)

Making up.
Prepare the florets, stitch the completed florets to the middle sized hexagons
and prepare the large base floret. Using **iron-on** *Vilene* instead of papers,
apply a central hexagon to each of the diamonds. Sew the diamonds around
the edge of the central floret.
Make up the cushion.

Key

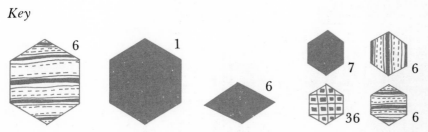

6   1   6   7   6

36   6

Cushion J

Size: 400 mm (16 in.) square when finished.

Prepare
16 square papers 100 mm (4 in.) sides. 8 light and 8 dark.
The ladder and numbers are made from tape.
Ladder 280 mm (11 in.). Rungs 50 mm (2 in.).
Make the paper for the snake from **iron-on** *Vilene*.

Apply the tape numbers to the patches before preparing the patches
(remember to cut the fabric for the patches larger than the measurement for
the papers).
Prepare the patches and sew them together.
Iron the 'paper' for the snake onto the wrong side of the satin and cut the
snake out allowing 12 mm (½ in.) turnings.
Tack the turnings down and sew the snake into place on the cushion.
Prepare the ladder and sew it into place.
Sew the backing onto the cushion.

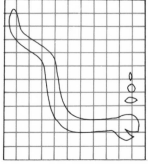

1 square = 1 in.

Cushion K

Size 400 mm (16 in.) square when finished.

Materials
½ m (½ yd) patterned fabric (back of patchwork and back of cushion)
Large scraps of patterned fabrics (2 patterns)
Large scraps of plain fabrics (2 colours)

Patches
Cut the ½ m (½ yd) of fabric into 2 pieces, each measuring 425 mm (17 in.) square
Cut 2 squares of patterned fabric, one 125 mm (5 in.) and one 225 mm (9 in.)
Cut 2 squares of plain fabric, one 312 mm (12¼ in.) and one 162 mm (6⅝ in.)
Turn 12 mm (½ in.) turnings on all but the largest squares
Position the squares as shown and stitch them down, smallest to largest.
Make up the cushion.

Cushion L

Size: 400 mm (16 in.)

Materials
½ m (½ yd) ticking
½ m (½ yd) backing fabric cut to 2 432 mm (17 in.) squares
½ m (⅓ yd) plain fabric
Large scraps of fabric in 3 different patterns.

Patches
From the plain fabric cut 4 strips each 350 mm (14 in.) long and 50 mm
(2 in.) wide and a square with 241 mm (9½ in.) sides.
Cut the ticking into a square with 330 mm (13 in.) sides.
Prepare 4 strips of patterned fabric each 200 mm (8 in.) long and 50 mm
(2 in.) wide.
Prepare a patterned square with 133 mm (5¼ in.) sides and another with
100 mm (4 in.) sides.

Making up
Make 12 mm (½ in.) turnings on all the pieces except for the ticking and the
backing square.
Starting with the smallest square, stitch the pieces down as shown.
Mount the finished patchwork onto one of the 432 mm (17 in.) backing
squares and make up the cushion.

Cushion M

Size 400 mm (16 in.)

Materials
¾ m (¾ yd) plain fabric
Scraps of patterned fabric
Made up cushion cover 400 mm (16 in.) square
25 small beads.

Making up
Make up the patchwork using a basic 225 mm (9 in.) square
Mount the patchwork onto the cushion cover and sew the small beads onto
the patchwork at all the points where the curves meet.

Cushion N Double rose point

Size: 400 mm (16 in.)

Materials
1 m (1 yd) plain fabric (pale)
⅓ m (⅓ yd) plain fabric (dark)
¼ m (¼ yd) patterned fabric
½ m (½ yd) plain fabric (for back of the cushion)
Tear the pale plain fabric into 225 mm (9 in.) squares and the dark plain fabric into 120 mm (4¾ in.) squares.
Tear the patterned fabric into 63 mm (2½ in.) squares.

Making up
Make up the pale fabric squares into the basic rosepoint base but before turning the corners to the middle for the second time, insert the dark squares under them (6 mm (¼ in.) turnings on the edges of the dark squares). Add the insert squares and you will see the dark fabric showing as you turn the pale fabric back over the insert squares.
Make up the cushion.

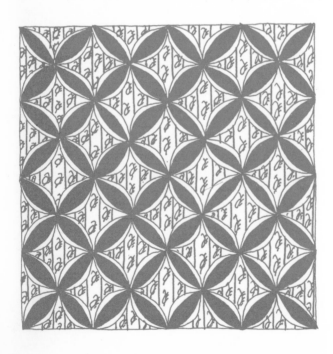

Pram quilt A

Size: 457 mm x 560 mm (18 in. x 22 in.)

Materials
1 m (1 yd) fabric 560 mm (22 in.) wide for backing
½ m (½ yd) wadding 560 mm (22 in.) wide
Large scraps of plain and patterned fabrics.

Patches
87 hexagonal papers made from a circle of 45 mm (1⁷⁄10 in.) radius.

Making up
Make up 62 striped patches and 25 plain patches.
Trim the wadding to 445 mm x 548 mm (17½ in. x 21½ in.).
Trim the backing fabric to 457 mm x 560 mm (18 in. x 22 in.). Fold
exactly in half and press to mark the centre. Press the half which is to
form the upper side into quarters.
Make up the patchwork and sew to the upper side. Press. Fold the fabric
in half again and stitch all round three sides, leaving an opening.
Insert the wadding through the opening.
Close the fourth side.
Working on a flat surface, tack all round the patchwork. Machine stitch over
the tacking and then remove tacking stitches.

Pram quilt B

Size: 457 mm x 560 mm (18 in. x 22 in.)

Materials
1 m (1 yd) backing fabric 560 mm (22 in.) wide
½ m (½ yd) wadding, trimmed to 445 x 548 mm (17½ x 21½ in.)
½ m (½ yd) pale grey cotton
½ m (½ yd) dark grey cotton
Scraps of black, white and yellow cotton fabric
½ m (½ yd) **iron-on** *Vilene*
Black sewing cotton
Draw up the graph (overleaf) full size, cut out the pieces and use them as patterns
to cut out the *Vilene* pieces. Cut the stripes freehand from scraps of *Vilene*.

Making up
Iron the *Vilene* onto the fabrics, leaving at least 25 mm (1 in.) between the
pieces.
Body, head, inner ears, legs, tail and feet: pale grey
Muzzle, ears and stripes: dark grey
Eyes: white. Inner eyes: yellow. Pupils: black.
Snip into any curved edges and turn the edges over the *Vilene* and tack down.

Assemble the cat in the following order:
Tail stripes onto the tail, body stripes onto the body, leg stripes onto the legs, head stripes onto the head, nose onto the muzzle, pupils onto the inner eye, inner eye onto the eye, muzzle onto the head, eyes onto the head, inner ears onto the ears, ears onto the head, head onto the legs, legs onto the body, body onto the tail.

Mount the whole cat onto the backing fabric and assemble the quilt.

Quilt round the edges of the cat and 25 mm (1 in.) from the edge of the quilt.

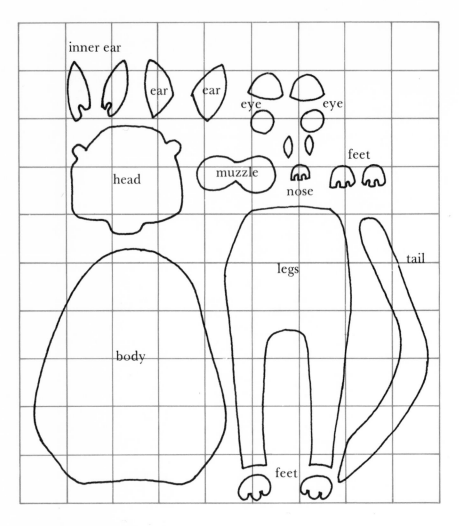

inner ear

ear

ear

eye

eye

head

muzzle

nose

feet

body

legs

tail

feet

1 square = 50 mm (2 in.)

40

Turtle quilt

Size 675 mm x 914 mm (23 in. x 35 in.)

Materials
1⅓ m (1½ yd) backing fabric (beige)
⅔ m (⅔ yd) wadding, trimmed to 663 mm x 902 mm (22½ in. x 24 in.)
3¼ m (3¼ yd) satin ribbon 75 mm (3 in.) wide.
⅓ m (⅓ yd) dark brown fabric
¼ m (¼ yd) mid brown fabric.

Prepare the patches. As for the cat quilt.
Body, face, inner scales and toenails: dark brown
Shell scales, legs, tail, head, eyelids and eyes: pale brown
Inner eyes: white. Pupils: black.

Assemble the turtle in this order
Scales s onto h. h and scales i onto a. a onto legs and tail. r onto q. q onto o.
p onto o.
Toenails k onto c. l onto e. m onto b. n onto d.
Eyes onto face, face onto head, body onto head.
Quilt the large shell scales.
Make up the quilt as shown on page 39.
Bind the edges of the quilt with the ribbon and quilt round the turtle and
along the inner edge of the ribbon.

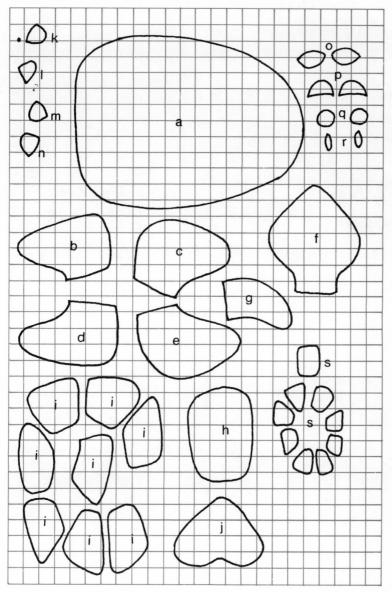

1 square = 25 mm (1 in.)

43

Alphabet cot quilt

Size: 700 mm x 950 mm (24 in. x 32 in.)

Materials
1¼ m (1⅓ yd) backing fabric 1·37 m (54 in.) wide
7½ m (8½ yd) 50 mm (2 in.) ribbon
¾ m (¾ yd) **iron-on** *Vilene*
Scraps of fabric both patterned and plain.
Wadding ⅔ m (⅔ yd) trimmed to 688 mm x 938 mm (23½ in. x 31½ in.)
Draw up the graphs to full size, cut the graph pieces out in **iron-on** *Vilene*
and press onto the fabrics. Tack the turnings.

Letters — use gingham and striped patterns.

Duck 1
Body: white. Wings, beak and feet: yellow. Legs and inner eye: orange.
Outer eye: red.
Make up the duck in this order:
f onto g. b onto a, a onto d, d onto c, e onto a.

Fish 2
Body: green. Fins and tail: darker green. Lateral stripe: orange. Outer eye:
orange. Inner eye: red. Buddles: blue.
Make up the fish in this order:
h onto g, a onto b and c (c is upside down on the graph), f, d, e and g onto a.
Bubbles onto the backing square.

Cat 3
Body, tail and head: grey. Chin, legs and outer ears: darker grey. Inner eye:
yellow. Pupils and nose: black.
Make up the cate in this order:
b onto a (cut curve and overlap as in the quilt drawing). e onto b, c onto e,
d onto c, h onto g, g onto f, f onto c, j behind the body.

Penguin 4
Body: black. Chest: white. Feet and beak: orange. Legs, outer eye and face:
pink. Wings: white. Wing edges: black.
Assemble the penguin in this order:
b onto a, d onto c, a onto c, a onto f, f onto e, j onto i, i onto a, g onto a,
and h onto a.

Turtle 5
Body, head, legs and tail: light green. Scales, eyelids and toenails: dark
green. Eyes: yellow.
Assemble the turtle in this order:
a onto b, d, c, and e. i, j, k and l, m onto a. h onto g. g onto e. toenails onto
legs.

Owl 6
Body: grey. Wings and feet: brown. Ears: dark brown. Outer eye and beak:
yellow. Inner eye: black.
Assemble the owl in this order:
b and c onto a. a onto d. a onto h. g onto f. f onto a. i onto a.

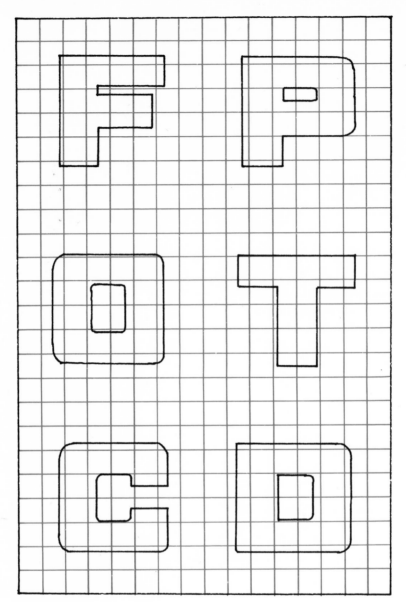

1 square = 25 mm (1 in.)

Assembling the quilt
Trim the backing fabric into a piece (25 in. x 33 in.) and 12 pieces, each
225 mm (9 in.) square.
Sew all the prepared letters and animals onto the squares of backing fabric.
Join up the squares as shown on page 44. Sew the ribbon round the edges of
each letter square.

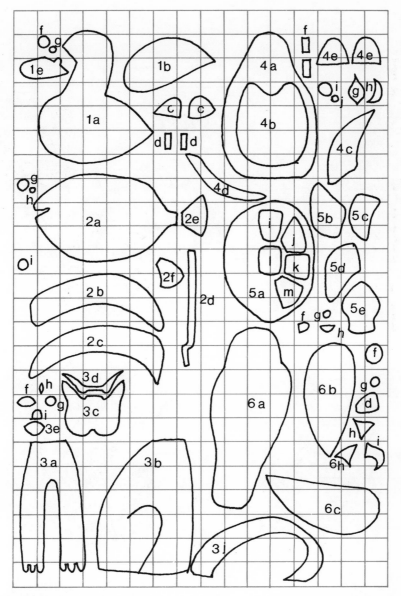

1 square = 25 mm (1 in.)

Sew the quilt front to the large piece of backing fabric round 3 sides and insert the wadding. Close the fourth side and quilt along the lines between the squares. Bind the edge of the quilt with ribbon.

Single quilt A

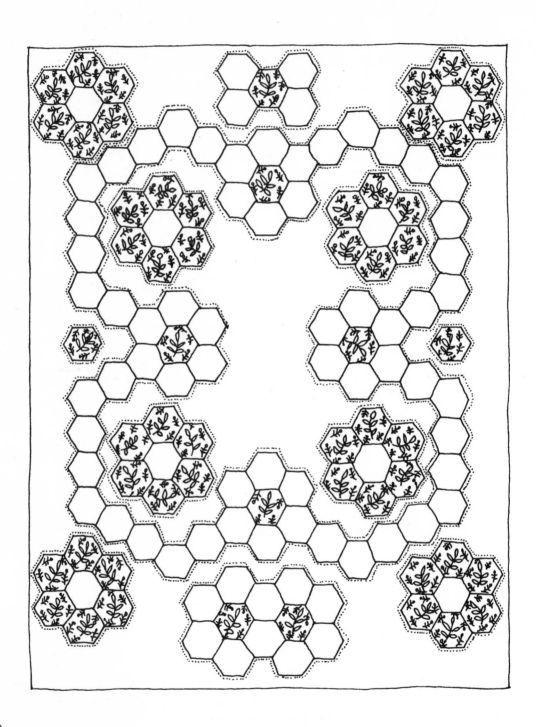

Size: approximately 2 m x 2·58 m (6 ft x 8 ft 6 in.)

Materials
Two double sheets each at least 2 m x 2·6 m (6 ft x 8 ft 6 in.)
1⅞ m (2 yd) patterned fabric
2½ m (2⅔ yd) plain fabric
A double blanket for the padding.

Patches
Prepare 129 papers. Make the hexagons from 88 mm (3½ in.) radius circles.
Prepare 57 patterned patches and 72 plain papers.

57   82

Making up
Join the patches as shown. Crease the backing fabric vertically and centre
the patchwork on it. Pin and tack the patchwork in place. Machine stitch
the patchwork down.
Place the layers of the quilt together, sandwiching the blanket between them.
Quilt round the edge of the patchwork and close the edges of the quilt.

Single quilt B

Size: 1·83 m x 2·44 m (6 ft x 8 ft)

Materials
1½ m (1½ yd) plain cotton pale
1½ m (1½ yd) plain cotton dark
1½ m (1½ yd) gingham
2⅓ m (2⅓ yd) wadding trimmed to 1·80 m x 2·41 m (71 in. x 95 in.)
2⅓ m (2⅓ yd) backing fabric trimmed to 1·83 m x 2·4 m (72 in. x 96 in.)
There are no papers for this quilt.

Making up

Cut or tear the plain cottons into squares with 279 mm (13 in.) sides.
Prepare 24 dark squares and 24 light squares.
Cut or tear the gingham into 48 squares with 241 mm (9½ in.) sides.
Make 12 mm (½ in.) turnings round all the edges of the gingham squares.
Centre the gingham squares diagonally on the dark and light squares.
Stitch them down.
Join the dark and light squares in a checkerboard pattern.
Make up the quilt and quilt along the lines between the dark and light squares.

Single quilt C

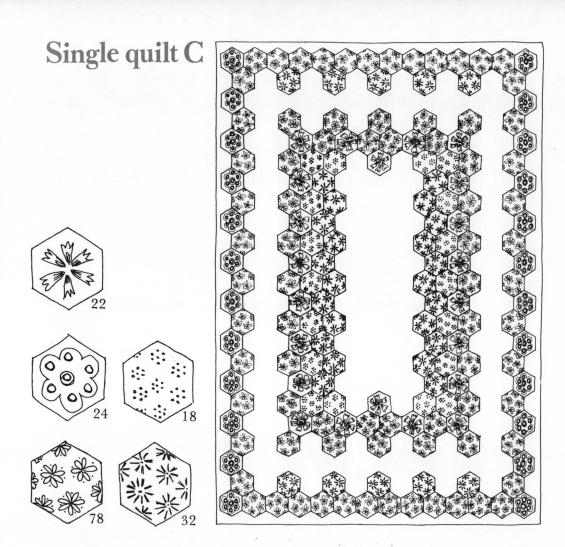

Size: approximately 2 m x 1⅜ m (78 in. x 55 in.)

Materials
3¼ m (3½ yd) sheeting trimmed to 3·84 m x 2·28 m (112 in. x 80 in.)
Large scraps of 5 different patterned fabrics.
1½ m (1½ yd) wadding, trimmed to 1·95 m x 1·38 m (77 in. x 54 in.)
Prepare 174 hexagonal papers using a 350 mm (2⅜ in.) circle.

Patches
Prepare the patches as shown on the patch key.

Making up
Join up the patchwork and mount it onto half of the fabric.
Make up the quilt and insert the wadding. Quilt around the edges of the
patchwork.

Single duvet cover

Size: 2 m x 1⅜ m (78 in. x 55 in.)

Materials
3¼ m (3½ yd) backing fabric 2·30 m (90 in.) wide. Trim to 2 m x 1⅜ m (78 in. x 55 in.)
1¼ m (1¼ yd) black fabric 1·21 m (45 in.) wide
1 m (1 yd) patterned fabric 1·21 m (45 in.) wide
⅝ m (⅝ yd) patterned fabric 1·21 m (45 in.) wide
⅓ m (⅓ yd) plain dark fabric 1·21 m (45 in.) wide
¼ m (¼ yd) plain pale fabric 1·21 m (45 in.) wide
Prepare the papers and patches as shown on the key.
Join the patches as shown and mount them onto the duvet cover.

Key
182 patches

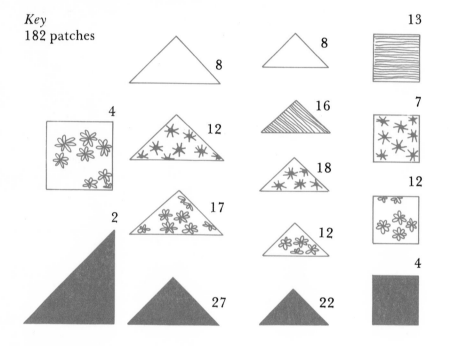

1 254 mm (10 in.) divided diagonally into halves (2)
16 squares 254 mm (10 in.) divided diagonally into quarters (64)
9 squares 254 mm (10 in.) divided horizontally and vertically into quarters quarters (36)
4 178 mm (7 in.) squares (4)
38 127 mm (5 in.) squares divided diagonally into halves (76)

Making up a duvet cover
Fold the fabric in half along the longest side. Apply the patchwork to one half.

Make a double turned edge along the two short sides and sew straight tape ties at 230 mm (9 in.) intervals down the short sides. Working right side out, join the edges at the top and bottom making a 12 mm (½ in.) seam, turn the cover right side in and sew the top and bottom edges again taking a slightly larger seam allowance. Turn right side out.

53

Double quilt   Houses

Size: 1·844 m (6 ft 6 in.) square

Materials
Backing fabric 2⅙ m (2⅙ yd) single sheeting
Sky ⅓ m (⅓ yd) blue sheeting
Sea ½ m (½ yd) greenish blue sheeting
Top field ⅓ m (⅓ yd) pale green sheeting
Lower field ½ m (½ yd) dark green sheeting
Houses 1 m (1 yd) each of pink and white sheeting

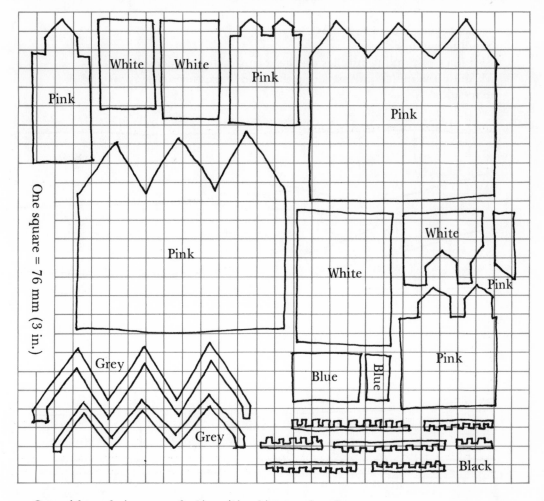

Quayside and zigzag roofs ½ m (½ yd) grey sheeting
Roofs ½ m (½ yd) brick coloured sheeting
Window panes, scraps of white and pale blue satin
Tape for the window bars 14 m (16 yd) of 25 mm (1 in.) tape.
½ m (½ yd) black fabric for the brick edgings.
Iron-on interlining 5m (5 yd)

The pattern
Scale up the graph pattern to full size and cut out all the pieces in interlining, cut 1 of everything except for the windows and doors, cut 6 windows
a, 7 windows b, 8 windows c, 12 windows d and 2 windows e. Cut 3 doors.
Iron the interlining papers onto the fabrics and cut the fabrics out, leaving
12 mm (½ in.) turnings.
Tack the edges of the patches down.
Assemble the quilt in the following order:
Sky, upper field, lower field. Assemble each house individually. (House, roof,
gables, brick edges windows) and then place the houses in position (rear
houses, insert steps and archway). Front houses (insert steps and archway),

sea and quayside (insert steps).
Sew the patches down.
Sew lines of running stitches on the sea using light green silk.
Make up the quilt, quilting along the field lines, the zigzag roofs and the
quaysides.

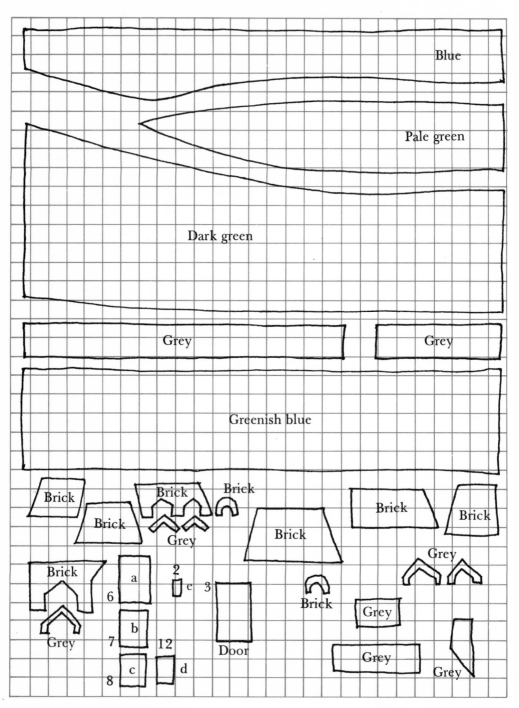

Double quilt Hexagons

Size: approximately 1·836 m x 2·140 m (6 ft 3 in. x 7 ft 3 in.)

Key

218	180	124	70	194	52	10	20

Materials
Backing fabric 2¼ m (2¼ yd) single sheeting
Patch fabrics, large quantities of fabric scraps.

Papers
Prepare 868 papers using a 102 mm (4 in.) circle

Patches   *See key*
Assemble the patches as shown, working from the centre.
Remove the papers and mount onto the backing fabric.

Double quilt Tulip pattern

Size: 2·149 m (7 ft 6 in.) square

Materials
4 ⅔ m (5 yd) single sheeting
2½ m (2½ yd) wadding, 2·149 m (90 in.) wide
Deep pink cotton. 1¼ m (1¼ yd)
Pale pink cotton ⅔ m (⅔ yd)
Mid pink cotton 1 m (1 yd)
Pale green cotton ¼ m (¼ yd)
5 m (5 yd) 50 mm (2 in.) pale green bias tape.
3 m (3 yd) iron-on interfacing.

Papers
Make these from the interlining, cut 13 of each pattern (grid overleaf)
Iron the pattern pieces onto the interfacing
a deep pink
b mid pink
c pale pink
d pale green
Cut the fabrics out leaving a turning allowance.
Tack the edges down and assemble each tulip.
Cut the backing fabric into 2 pieces and stitch the tulips onto the fabric as
shown.

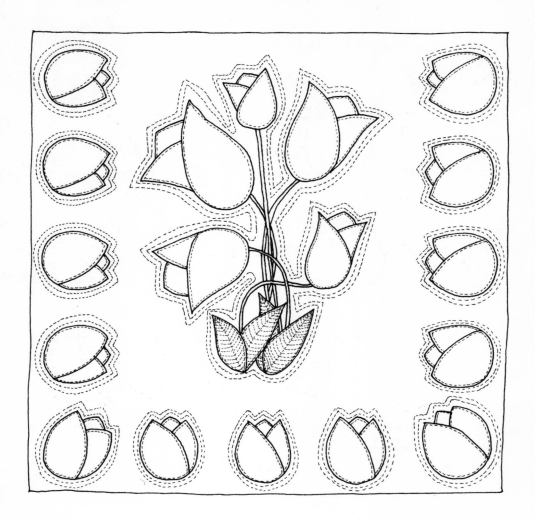

Make up the quilt and quilt round the edges of the applied tulips.
The stems are made from bias binding.

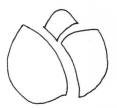

Cut 13 of each of these
See grid overleaf

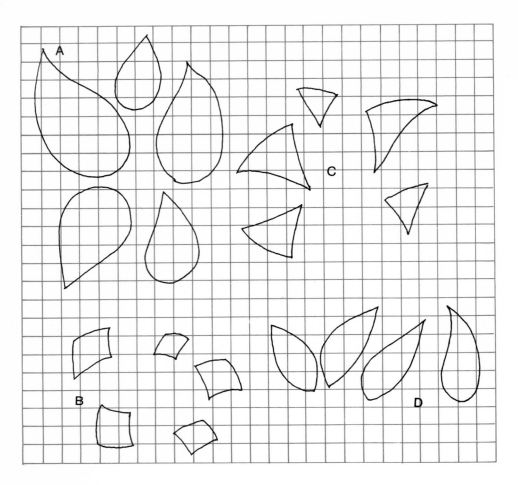

1 square = 76 (3 in.)

Double onlaid quilt

Size: 1·844 m x 2·133 m (6 ft 6 in. x 7 ft)

Key

 A

 B

 C   Plain dark D

Plain light E

Materials

Backing fabric 2¾ m (2⅝ yd) single sheeting

Fabric A (*see key*)
1⅓ m (1½ yd) fabric 1:235 m (54 in.) wide

Fabric B
⅔ m (⅔ yd) fabric

Fabric C
⅔ m (⅔ yd)

Fabric D
½ m (½ yd)

Fabric E
3⅓ m (3⅓ yd)

Cutting the pieces

A   Cut into a square with 1·235 m (54 in.) sides

B   Cut into a square with 9144 mm (36 in.) sides and 4 squares with 432 432 mm (18 in.) sides

C   Cut into a square with 335 mm (13 in.) sides and 4 squares with 229 mm (9 in.) sides

D   Cut into a square with 432 mm (18 in.) sides

E   Cut into strips 254 mm (10 in.) wide
(30 strips)   6 strips 9169 mm (37 in.) long
20 strips 3251 mm (20 in.) long
4 strips 1235 mm (54 in.) long

Turn a 12 mm (½ in) turning on all the strips and round the 5 smallest squares.

Assemble the quilt as shown in the diagram.

Stockists Great Britain

Templates
Mary Jackson
Churchtown
Southport, Lancashire

J. E. M. Patchwork Templates
Watlington, Oxfordshire, and
Forge House, 18 St Helen's Street
Cockermouth, Cumberland

A. M. Row and Son Limited
42 Market Place, Ripon, Yorks

Vilene
Obtainable from most
department stores

Threads and accessories
E. J. Arnold (School Suppliers)
Butterley Street, Leeds LS10 1AX

Art Needlework Industries Ltd
7 St Michael's Mansions
Ship Street, Oxford

*The Campden Needlecraft
Centre*
High Street
Chipping Campden
Gloucestershire

Craftsman's Mark Limited
Broadlands, Shortheath
Farnham, Surrey

Dryad
Northgates, Leicester LE1 4QR

Fresew
97 The Paddocks
Stevenage SG2 9UQ
Hertfordshire

Hugh Griffiths
Brookdale, Beckington
Bath, Somerset

J. Hyslop Bathgate and Company
Victoria Works, Galashiels

Mace and Nairn
89 Crane Street, Salisbury, Wilts

The Needlewoman Shop
146 Regent Street, London W1

Nottingham Handcraft Company
(School Suppliers) Melton Road
West Bridgford, Nottingham

Christine Riley
53 Barclay Street, Stonehaven
Kincardineshire AB3 2AR

The Silver Thimble
33 Gay Street
Bath

Elizabeth Tacy
45 High Street
Haslemere, Surrey

Joan L. Trickett
110 Marsden Road
Burnley, Lancashire

Stockists USA

Threads and accessories

American Crewel Studio
Box 553 Westfield
New Jersey 07091

American Thread Corporation
90 Park Avenue, New York

The Golden Eye
Box 205
Chestnut Hill
Massachusetts 02167

Lily Mills
Shelby
North Carolina 28150

Nettie's Needlecraft
200 N. Indian Avenue
Palm Springs
California 92262

The Thread Shed
307 Freeport Road
Pittsburgh, Pennsylvania 15215

Yarncrafts Limited
3146 M Street
North West Washington DC

Pellon (US equivalent of *Vilene*)
Obtainable from most
department stores

Bibliography

Ideas for Patchwork Suzy Ives
Simple Patchwork Alice Timmins
Patchwork Averil Colby
Patchwork Quilts Averil Colby
Machine Stitches Anne Butler
Fun with Appliqué and Patchwork
Ilse Strobl-Wohlschläger
Inspiration for Embroidery
Constance Howard
Embroidery and Colour
Constance Howard

all published by B T Batsford
Limited